ODYSSEY CALLING

Vahni Capildeo

SAD PRESS
Bristol 2020

for Sveinn Haraldsson

CONTENTS

Holy Island	1
beginnings of bluegreen: Azure Noise and Kinetic Syntax	2
beginnings of bluegreen: Spindrift Silences	6
Odyssey Response	7
Windrush Reflections	15
A Short Prayer to Coffee, which Crosses the Sea	26
Landfall	28
In Praise of Birds	29
A Short Prayer to Oceans, by Erasures	34
Acknowledgements	35

Holy Island

The wind is high today.

The seals are hiding under rocks.

The seals have gone to the other islands.

Come back this afternoon.

Listen for the seals.

What do they sound like?

They sound like ghosts.

beginnings of bluegreen

I.   Azure Noise and Kinetic Syntax: Poetry as a Space of Active Silence

In a series of experiments with breaking away from poems on the page to create immersive installations, I have been seeking to re-create what the process of enjoying reading or writing poetry feels like. A habit of concentration was given to me in childhood by poetry-loving folk; so I was always privileged to fall through a portal-like page, into worlds whose colour, sound and movement momentarily displaced everything. However, reading is not like this for everyone. It is easy to blank at the sight of a poem, reject it as 'too personal', or agonize over its 'meaning'. Its words may not whisper or sing; the mistrustful imagination voices them like a tired performer mumbling in a marquee, or a strident teacher. So I desired to create active silence in a room filled with happy concentration. The intention was not to abandon the poem, nor to illustrate it, but to offer a magic gift: a relaxed, humming brain-cave you can step into.

Who can explain this feeling intellectually? What it feels like, after learning by heart, reading aloud, copying by hand, analyzing at length, even or especially writing that you *don't* 'like' or 'get' – to acquire the technical ease of slipping fearlessly into the deeps of a poem?

'Azure Noise', playing both on 'white noise' and Mallarmé's poetry-ships sailing into the symbolic *azur*, was the title of one instantiation, co-created with Jeremy Hardingham, the genius manager of the Judith E. Wilson Drama Studio. Our soundscape's word-shimmer would invite the audience to unplug and re-tune, unravelling the worried, mediatized buzz of everyday modernity. We selected texts with round vowels and liquids, or mentions of blue-green colours, mirrors, ice, and water. These included contemporary Latin American and Caribbean poetry, medieval Welsh, Ursula Le Guin, Angela Carter, and my *Undraining Sea*. We layered recordings featuring diverse volunteer readers, and placed four devices playing different soundtracks at different points in the studio. Because only occasional words rose to the surface, listeners were encouraged to enter a dreamlike state, open to wandering with and into poetic meaning rather than wrestling with 'correct' responses. The shifting interzones of murmurs, just under hearing level, positively countered the noise that public spaces enforce.

After sound, the second key element was movement. We developed a 'kinetic syntax' approach, also intended to unlock the living feel of poems, rather than what they seem to talk about. In this approach, interpretative gestures, such as river = wavy arms, were banned. Instead, Jeremy's core response would make visible shapes that could convey the feeling of the small movements that add up to the sense of how a text is creatively formed. We analyzed our texts down to their linguistic skeletons. Phrases or fragments? Lines – run-on or end-stopped? Verb tenses – changing, past, present, infinitive? Grammatical structures, repetitions? What was 'dancing' in the language, through the *if, or, when, then, and, but, O!* – not the *who* and *what?* This liberated his viewers to 'dance with' the poetry, becoming empathetic rather than being trapped in literalism.

Time and space remained to arrange. Not everyone pays poetic attention when they have to listen 'properly'. Some people need to move about or to make or even destroy something, to access that zone of feeling and/both, switched on/switched off.

To break the association between poetry and school discipline, we decided the audience could drop in and out any time during a four-hour continuous performance. They were not required to be well-behaved spectators. So we placed mattresses and sheeting on the floor, to encourage lounging; chairs facing various directions; and objects to play or make art with.

Swathes of fabric: velvety, translucent, netted, slippery, blue, silvery, green: hammocked and hummocked the 'black box'. Paige Smeaton, with expertise carried over from Ceredigion Museum, provided the focal point in the entrance sightline, slowly metamorphosing into a Mabinogion bird. Along the studio's left wall was a corridor of mesmeric motion. Olivia Scott-Berry, hooded and facing away, repurposed bills and receipts, painting them with shapes like drowsy waterfowl. Hope Doherty, like the sellers of holy items on the causeway to a Sufi shrine, had a stall of simple, lustrous things: beads, marbles in water-filled Ziploc bags. She made non-stop, gentle offerings, like a happy Ophelia drowning among her wares. Along the right wall Jeremy Hardingham evolved a barefoot fire and water ritual. Meantime, hidden on a platform, I read water poems clearly, but softly, so the audience could choose their level of engagement. This was the creation of active silence. Few would go away with 'a meaning', but with the memory of an enriching atmosphere, and perhaps, imperceptibly, a little changed in their access and approach to poetry.

beginnings of bluegreen

II. Spindrift Silences

Listen. Blue. The flow of blue capillaries. Sleepy fish, all blue in their flight. In the dark room, only you. Sounds melt away, strengthening silence, sometimes admitting dumbfounded, liquid words in music. For my sake, the folds of your wound soften enough to become water. Time passes. You can hear falling snow watering the blue of the sea. Deeper water. Emptier silence. Susurrus. Only you cry a thousand treasurable cries, wetnosed as a swimmer. The crevasse, dark subtle wound, extended beyond dark silver, all blue drift, all blue drink, gateway joy. *Lauluaa*. Sometimes outsider status drops expected but absent barriers. Their dreams winced, webfoot in the middle of the big seas. Perhaps silver flooded and lulled glass vessels, forming the bell only you received, sleeping in quicksands. Time passes, and drops the keystone in the arch.

ODYSSEY RESPONSE

I. Words, take wing

Words, take wing, fly commonly among all people
who have power of health and employment over us;
go like the sparrows rife on summer streets of a holy
island; unlearn any fear; flitting, bring to mind
light, and how quickly light fades; bring to mind life,
comfort in houses, fragile as windows onto space.
Words, take wing, as if lawyers were angels, as if death
were a paper doll in a set of identical
paper dolls, an infinite set of paper doll kings
of terror, cancelled by a gentle fiery sword.
Sometimes, words, you launch in many lovely languages; yet,
before you begin to fly, you are misrecognized,
like an owl entering a superstitious person's
open-plan room being beaten to death, Athena's
wise bird struck down, bloody feathers everywhere,
a soft body a futile piñata
releasing clouds. Could you gather up a faith
in strangers, in the absence of a god of strangers?
Does any homeless person gleam like a god in disguise?
Disgust rules. Do without. Doing without big symbols.
Zeus! Eagles may acquire cruel associations.
Words, take wing, fly commonly among all people
who share vulnerability on a trembling earth;
who drink, or hope to drink, sweetly, cool water.

II. Hero?

Tell me how to simplify a song. Tell me about
identity; fidelity. Solve the problem of a face.
Tell me about a state governed by emotion – would you move?
Choose to move? If they force you into moving?
If you cannot afford to, cannot afford not to –
Make a song about one person. Who can cope.
    Is it a hero you want? Why not say so?
I am suspicious of heroes. How do they survive?
I know a mother who scattered her children
on the way out of war, and has not gone back to look.
What if the hero shining like a falcon arrives
having traded their body for life, trailing killings
and transactional sex? Is the hero empowered
to treat their spouse to raw cuts of trauma, treat them worse
and better than anyone else? Help can be a trap.
Home, a mating of traps. Who do you want at your back?
Enough. I am privileged to have civil conversations
in a corrected city, commemorate the correct dead.
    How changeable is a hero, like modern rainfall patterns.
How fearful is a hero, patched like an archaic sail.
How lifted up is a hero, like the great-grandchild
of immigrants, hurting his parents, hoping his child is kind.
Witness those ghosts who, after a natural disaster, don't know
they're dead; poor, wet ghosts, trying to board real taxis home.

III. The sea

Hooves, chevrons, arrowheads, champion ski racers, nothing, no,
nothing runs so swiftly, nothing seems to run so, so
swiftly as cool water pours back in, making
an island of a piece of land once, sometimes, no more
than another part of the shore, a tidal island.
Nothing runs so swiftly. Did you think I was singing
about death? Should we give death preferential treatment?
Should we be women singing to death? You saw. You know.
The sea is a cover for bones, how busyness covers news.
New bodies are laid every day in the innocence
of the sea. New burdens explode every day
in the innocence of the air. How many
of my family dropped like shining falcons
in the duress of a forced migration, ivorying
into the sunken halls of the only Atlantis
really worthy of the name? The sea is a cover.
There is a law of the sea – No. The sea is lawless.
There is a modern law of the sea. The conference
proceeded for nine years. – No. It is a convention
of the toothless, for the toothless, by the toothless.
The sea needs teeth. – How can there be freedom of the sea without protection? –
How can you be territorial about the sea?
Most of the civilized – America never agreed. Never –

IV. Companion

I tremble to think of meeting you. How did we meet
on this trembling earth?
    A blizzard blew up. We sat
on a stone, a few paces from the farmhouse.
We could not see, or move, to go to them. They could not
come to us. We could not discern the tide, rising towards us.
    How did we meet?
    He had turned his back on you. I loved
the poetry of your anger. I wanted the poetry
of your anger on my small island. Transported. Cherished.
Forget any other kind of kiss.
    I tremble to think of not meeting you. You could be
better off. Light was fading quickly. You saw. You knew
I was unsafe, waiting, in my full-passported femaleness
in the cruel associations of a village
of privileged abandonment. You sat on the bench,
reached beyond death into Persia at your back,
unrolled for me a mat of pure imagination,
placed for us both a vase of pure imagination.
Your metamorphosis was from refugee to host.
In the street, you gathered guest-right, offered me
hospitality where had been others' hostility, till
my neglectful, official friend arrived. We thrived, like two birds
in an embroidery orchard of pomegranates, oranges,
and weeping pears: like impossibilities of climate
redemption.
    They spin epic words to say none of this is home.

V. Hades Social

Be thankful for the friends in a blue and white country
who invite you to meet their dead. Together, in a small group,
crossing the clean-smelling river pierced by mossy rocks,
enter among tombs like garden sheds, houses;
graves with lost names, granite pitted by acid rainfall patterns.
Rub flowerless hands over lost names. – Try not to bring
anyone home with you, someone invisible says
in your memory, sharpening into many voices,
women singing to death.
 What is this place? How did you get here?
You know. Graveyards are unclean. The only way to go
is by fire open to the sky, on fragrant woods,
white camphor tucked under your tongue, releasing spirit
from the ragged body to the innocence of air.
– I cannot be burnt, I cannot burn as I need to
burn, among these new friends, these kind friends, thinks the stranger.
Be glad to meet the new kind dead your friends have buried. You saw.
Next time bring flowers. – But I am sad for my future,
in a country where my funeral customs are illegal.
Whose problem is a soul? Identity? Fidelity? Death
is a thief in a stationery shop. He strolls out.
The shopkeeper, a poor man, runs after, shouting. – I saw you!
Give that back! – Give back what? Death says, strolling out.
Hermes is a tram attendant who holds your coffee,
helping you find the coin you dropped; it rolls underfoot.

VI. The faces of Odysseus

When the trembling earth dips away from our common ancestor,
a wife living as a widow may look at the streaks and stripes
of another seaside sunset, beauty in isolation,
and tremble like the earth at the men lined up
to land on her like shining falcons, quickly, but not lightly.
If an old person perseveres in life, yet needing your care,
do not harass or tease them as Odysseus did,
tricking his father into hardworking tears, washing his brain
with real grief and reactive gladness.
You know, you see Christ in the face of a wounded enemy,
if you listen to the now-celebrated poets weeping.
What if you hear the song of yourself simplified on the news?
What if your song is impermissible as the blacked-out news?
Odysseus, I see you. I know I thought I might
dislike you. You were so hot. You planned it: standing naked, hot,
in the doorway, drawing the long bow no-one else could.
Standing where Penelope could see the slaughter of fine men
her hero would commit, war for an indoor Helen.
I see you in the face of the vagrant thoughtfully
washing his clothes at the standpipe in the Savannah
under the trees with no-one to care. No-one, Odysseus.
One man's soldier is another man's beggar, Odysseus.
He lives without love or teasing, sweet talk or complication.
One woman's king is another woman's case, Odysseus.

VII. Zeus, god of strangers

Stranger, how are you cast away, cast upon your own
resources, cast on wildly different styles of hosting?
What if your angry host feeds you up to go to war?
What if the gifts lavished on you lay expectations on you
to go away, make a success of yourself, and don't come back?
What if you are blown back, empty-handed? You would be
right to hide your name. Yes? You are a king at home. No?
Slaughter and laughter cross your threshold
in your absence. Slaughter and laughter at a distance
shadow and echo you, no matter how you set off,
or your clean presentation, now, among the élite. Yes? No?
Where are you? Islands aren't always islands. All maps are pop-up.
Volcanos yawn, spatter out something the sea covers over.
Rivers rise, or silt up. Clumps form, or dissolve, barely the size
for two blue-coated Norsemen to duel on.
Islands are provisional. World; whirl. The sea covers over.
The Queen of the Dead lifts, in her lily hand
with its violet nails, a head of snakehair.
Do not go too deep. That way paralysis. You want action,
like tired people do. Stranger, you are cast like in a dream
of being on stage, unprepared. Is it right to invent lines?
Traveller in body, buffeted about as a guest, Zeus
loves us. Spirit Traveller, revive as a good host. By Zeus,
Time Traveller, if you see Columbus, shoot on sight.

VIII. That's epic

There is a city beneath the city beneath the city
beneath the floodplain. Forget about it. A city
is at the back of the city at the back of the city.
Ignore it. Ignore the scripts in which mathematics
and astronomy were first written. Ignore the scripts
incised in rock, the scripts inscribed in landscape.
O Muse, make the poet move on. Memory is no good
to triumphant civilizations.
O Muse, your poet is blind, saying life has a sheen.
O Muse, your poet's a hostage, saying land has a meaning.
Nobody likes a try-hard, a lacemaker working
with a vascular surgeon to join delicate gaps.
Put memory in the service of intention
to keep the story shining, like tears shed over onionskin,
or the cheering faces of the well-fed family watching
screensful of migrants plummeting or washed up
at a border, from a wall. The camera admires
guards, themselves descended from migrants.
The shining chorus of weaponry,
made manifest by taxes, drops death
on more children shining and their many lovely languages
as if they were done for from the get-go, like paper brochures
in a digital age. Forget about it.
Keep going. A story has the tricks of appetite.

WINDRUSH REFLECTIONS

I. Windrush Lineage

They came in earlier ships,
Mahadai's ancestors and mine,
with hope, and by imperialist design;
and I am too young to have seen them
dying, as she says, on streets.
I am resigned to dreaming them
wherever Victorian iron
palisades the public squares
like spears. I take her word
that the bread they died wanting
was British; the languages
and laws denied them were British,
for a quarter of the globe
rose pink to cry empire,
havoc, and natural resource.
　This was recent.
Recent enough: my cousin
saw them too. The finish
of those ships overlapping
as ships ineluctably do
with others, keening the curled
wake with a forward-looking wave.
　The sea is like this.
What you expect nobody
can expect. What you accept
nobody can't accept.

What the great hungry puzzle
stamped with a crown is
must be big enough to see
big enough to ignore.
  Why wouldn't you
take a canoe, a pirogue,
carrack, caravel, ocean
liner, yacht, banana boat,
naval destroyer, oil tanker
or cruise ship, why wouldn't you?
When survival becomes
an acquired taste, improvement
a second skin, and home
is a long-distance love affair
with loss, and home is an arranged
marriage to glorious, unseen London?
  Windrush wasn't the first.
The voyage was not an arrow
flying one way to lodge in sorrow.
Island people met island
people on the docks. Some were there
long time. Some stayed. Some went back.
Twelve to a room, cold in welcome,
post-war Britain already was home
by birthright: documentation
was not a prize or a promise
for this generation born under

the far-fetched Union Jack. Citizens
drilled in the hymns and nursery rhymes,
sweepings of a dust-devil map?
Singer, soldier, fabric designer,
novelist, nurse, BBC presenter,
stowaway, activist, carnival maker,
lawyer, bus driver, self-reinventor,
brought up as British in sightline and grip
crossing to Britain, the way some move
to Leeds from York. Surely. Sure. No more.
 Sugar brickwork, tobacco boulevards
and bloody wool are the well-known parts
making Albion's very groundsong
a subclass of Caribbean harmonies.
 It takes a special effort
to tune out the transatlantic
jumbie jumble ripple
in the Humber and the Thames.
Hear now: Lord Beginner. Lord
Kitchener. Sam Selvon. V.S. Naipaul.
Mikey Smith, stoned to death in Jamaica.
Una Marson, ruling the airwaves.
Wilson Harris. The nationality
act in one of its ever-revisable
revisions. And a prime minister,
and a journalist…

II.   Windrush Caribbean Cento

Things does have a way of fixing themselves.
Cyaan mek blood out a stone.
Be it enacted by the King's most Excellent Majesty,
one grim winter evening, when it had a kind of uneasiness about London;
by and with the advice of the Lords Spiritual and Temporal, and Commons
fury and diamond.
Is a place where everyone is your enemy and your friend,
or else like charcoal to grain.
An Act to make provision for British nationality.
I am glad to know my Mother Country.
Rest, then, my heart, thou knowest but too well
I an I alone.
Where I come from you take what you want
and you pay every Friday,
and for citizenship of the United Kingdom and Colonies.
But let me just look at what the policy…
Cricket lovely Cricket!
But I keep coming back to it:
Your hostile environment policy.
The compliant environment policy,
The government is taking action against
every person who under this Act is a citizen of the United Kingdom
and Colonies,
a dancing dwarf on the tarmac.

Spirit of leaves like smoke.
A burning injustice.
But our hearts are white.
A burning injustice.
But their hearts are black.
God is sen you His spirit,
Windrush.
This lady died.
Because the English people are very much sociable,
every person born within the United Kingdom and Colonies,
in the womb of converted horse
in the Christmas supplement of the colour magazine,
you're absolutely right,
shall be a citizen of the United Kingdom and Colonies by birth,
but as me gon in
cock-roach rat and scorpion also come in.
What is it that a city have
that any place in the world have...
room dem a rent.
Hate dat ironed hair.
He looked in the mirror one day
and couldn't see himself.
Citizenship by birth.
Citizenship by descent.
Citizenship by registration.
After all was said and done,
Birth is never treason.
And he began to scream.

You thinking about the thing without a name
You get so much to like it
you wouldn't leave it for anywhere else,
subject to the provisions of this section.
Second Test and the West Indies won.

III.   Windrush Exhibition

I fail the bag check. Once in,
my phone falls under suspicion.
It feels like pulling a string
when I give the names and the reason
that let me photograph the exhibition:
Songs of a Strange Land.
    There are no arrows. You make
your own way; excavate
your own gates. What is a keeper?
    The 1700s names and sale prices
for old to underage slaves
sold off with a Tobago estate...
But that is not Windrush 1948?
The footage of 2000s Brits driven out
for a retroactive lack of paperwork...
Is all Caribbean heritage Windrush?
    I miss the delight and taxonomy
of birds, woods, foods, medals or geology,
the ocean of non-human
lapping humanity.
    But here are voices
beyond glass cases: letters
between brothers, entertainments
in community magazines,
funerals and arrivals,
achievements, doubts and designs.

If only 'shock and awe' were a phrase
we could reclaim, not to mean 'war',
that might lift off with love, like good labels do.
   Can these stories, their satin and skulls,
good-clothes and cologne, like a Pierrot pun
or a Robber cloak, unfold unfurl unfall
their particular nuance, universal burn,
3ookm away as the egret flies
from London to south Leeds?
   It is not informational, it is
not a blameshift, it is not
all-lives-matter top down and sideways blank.
It is in itself important,
crucial in the crucible of history:
these isles and these isles
these shelves and these selves
these aisles and desires
these disasters and out of disasters
these stars and the astronomer out for stars…
If you could send a postcard
to the past, send a postcard
to the future, if you could
welcome, warn, object or anything else

that reaches flying, what would you, would you,
if you could, would you send, would you have
sent? You on the journeys from Ireland,
Bangladesh, Cumbria, you with different
literacies, you in the forest
of skilled restoration, achievements by your hand
and unsigned, you with the quick eye to sketch,
you on the everlasting buses?
You share your music and tell me
you'd take a calypsonian to lunch…

IV.　　Windrush Leeds Cento

Stay, if you've come all this way.
I also know about uprooting.
In the airport the smells were
mixed. Anxious. Friends
to lonely, what a journey.
Who did you leave behind?
Approach. Anxious. Someone
to love. A travel buddy.
You will be welcome here;
we finally settled.
How was the voyage?
Come here! I would
take you for a walk
and show you York. Leeds
Town Hall. Kirkgate Market.
Bradford. Chapeltown. Spain.
Blackpool. Windermere. Turkey.
Not everybody lives in Buckingham Palace.
I'd like to show you round
Leeds. Celebrate the NHS.
Dear Mr Churchill... Dear President
Kennedy... Getting experience
after unemployment. Nursing and tending
to old soldiers. Can't wait for peace
and quiet. In this big freezer.

Family near me.
Know the area. Explore. Enjoy.
I walk around the park
and I found a friend.
Please sing another song.

A Short Prayer to Coffee which Crosses the Sea

Prayer lurks in the uncertain air between poetry and philosophy, in the heat at the coppery base of the cezve, in the steam of the human breath meeting the haar of a northern morning where the sun rises orange over a bitter sea.

Witness this endeavour of faith in the poet Helen and the philosopher Aaron's Leeds coffee-house conversational book project. Additionally witness the accompanying assertions of faith, such as the faith in almonds, and the acts of faith accompanying these additional assertions of faith. Witness the extension of faith to California, a land whose existence remains unproven to me by experience: California also of oranges and salt water, California of wildfires, California of sequoias, California producer of eighty per cent of the world's almonds, a land of silica mines, fistfuls of protein, and air miles.

Prayer lurks in the agon of poetry and philosophy. Rejoice therefore, as if divinely caffeinated. Rejoice even in the side effects. Rejoice in the used grounds. Hosanna from the straw men of argument, rising like a struggle and reduced to streamers. Hosanna from the organs in subtle states of damage from false yoga, felt and undetected, hot, compressed, suffered, diagnosed. Hosanna from the souls of the insects and minerals crushed to make paint for gaudy Greek and Roman statues, before those icons were whitened for much later museums into the likeness of whitened cemeteries for much later colonizers' great wars.

Prayer lurks in the exalted origins of coffee on our originator continent; in the upraising of Yemen and the grandeur of Yemen's port of Mocha, original exporter of the brilliant beans and lender of its rich name to our lower-case blend named mocha; in the upraising of the intoxicating civilization of Ethiopia; the upraising of the sophisticated thirst of Egypt. Raise up these primary hosts of the world's coffee-houses. Praise to their early enliveners. Praise to the Sufi mystics, frequenters of the coffee-houses. Praise praise praise to the unnumbered branches and unusual grounds of their debates. Praise to the acerbic throat of the great grey wolf, the Ottoman Empire, popularizer of coffee to its tiny kittycat rival, Venice, Venice who played catchup by opening its own café in 1647, the first in the west.

Rest in blessed memory, Jacob, called 'the Jew' by an English diarist. Delurk from history how the newness of Jacob's business was also a return, three hundred and sixty years after the king expelled all Jews from England. Live, readers and coffee-drinkers, and think to praise the good taste of the modern-minded Jacob; hot on the heels of the Venetians, he opened England's first coffee-house, in 1651, in Oxford, that city where the learned reputedly talk and profess.

Landfall

whenever the sea
lies flat out, the deceiver
might well stand straight up

new roads old inlets
peak Dutch Englished for Scotland
a heaving haven

haar ambers the sun
three degrees all year rising
sky blue paint flakes off

for mending of nets
rubble stairs tower around
a fisheries floor

the standing lamp walks
an old convex mirror makes
a headed torso

how to name places
Scottish herring girls work still
in Norfolk stained glass

washed and emptied walls
need no washing emptying
to be washed empty

Edinburgh Ember
Ilion Illuvium
Iere & Iere

In Praise of Birds

In praise of high-contrast birds, purple bougainvillea thicketing the golden oriole.

In praise of civic birds, vultures cleansing the valleys, hummingbird logos on the tails of propeller planes; in praise of adaptable birds, the herring gull that demonstrates its knowledge of how to use a box junction, and seems to want to cross the road.

In praise of birds eaten by aeroplane engines; in praise of birds trained to hunt drones; in praise of birds that, having nothing to do with human processes, crash aeroplanes.

In praise of suicidal birds, brown ground doves forgetful of wingèdness, in front of cars, slowly crossing the road.

In praise of perse birds like fish smashing out of a bowl.

In praise of talk being cheep, and in praise of men who shut up about birds.

In praise of birds of death and communication, Garuda the almost-but-more-than-an-eagle vehicle of the darkly bejewelled and awfully laughing Lord of Death.

In praise of badly drawn birds.

In praise of white egrets, sitting on mud, hippos, and lines about old age.

In praise of Old English birds of exile, the gannet's laughter, swathes of remembered seabirds booming and chuckling, the urgent cuckoo blazing on about summer, mournful and mindblowing, driving the sailor over the edge towards impossible targets, scornful of gardens, salty about city life – I can't stand not setting off; far is seldom far enough.

In praise of a turn of good cluck.

In praise of the high-dancing birds carried on the heads of masqueraders and built by wirebenders to carry the spirit of an archipelago of more than seven thousand isles.

In praise of grackles quarrelling on the lawn.

In praise of unbeautiful birds abounding in Old Norse, language of scavenging ravens, thought and memory, a treacherous duo. The giantess down from the mountain complained – I couldn't sleep in a coastal bed because of the yammering of waterfowl. Every morning that blasted seagull wakes me.

In praise of the peacocks invading the car park at the Viking conference in York, warming their spread tails on the bodies of cars.

In praise of the early bird who liberates the dewy worm from glaucous grass.

In praise of birds of timetelling: green-rumped parrots for morning, kiskadees dipping at night: and the absence of birds of timetelling, the unreeled horror of humanly meaningless time.

In praise of the bird of the soul that flies out when the body is molested, and in praise of that bird recalling the abuse room as if perched on the highest point of the pinewood press.

In praise of the blueblack grassquit, which is inky and small.

In praise of the albatross, in praise of the double doors to a swimming baths hall.

In praise of birds of concussion, notes in the air being all the brain can cope with.

In praise of birds as edible and in praise of birds as angels and in praise of birds as stones and in praise of Thoth the Ibis.

In praise of the birds of climate change, forest warblers bringing a new song to the suburbs, late-leaving Arctic tern teenagers blizzarding the beach.

In praise of ducking and diving, and without praise of the cruelty of quills.

In praise of birds that are not punctuation, that are not calendars, that are not words.

In praise of birds that occupy and disrupt a lyrical musical staff.

In praise of birds that singing still do shit, shitting ever singing, above a low-rent skylight, on a diet of chips.

In praise of triangulation and three unseen corncrakes by whose calls guests may recognize the way to the house on the tipsy hill.

In praise of increasingly grotesque fossil remains of proto-birds, and the discovery of normality as never having been such.

In praise of birds plucked for dream armour, flame fur, plate plume, and in praise of women who fight like cranes and swans.

In praise of thump and slime.

In praise of fine feathers, prophecies, and export regulations.

In praise of Quetzalcoatl. Tremble to say more.

In praise of the birds of prognostication, gutted, magnetic, or altering their calls.

In praise of rare and less showy doctors refraining from labelling immigrants as insane or aggressive, as more regularly spotted doctors may be observed to do.

In praise of Suibhne, driven mad by the dinning of church bells, yearning for his dinner of unchlorinated cress.

In praise of Suibhne's flights crossing land and water, and Suibhne's poetry crossing time and language, to and from, tidalectic, praise.

A Short Prayer to Oceans, by Erasures

open formula	dark footsteps	blessing	freedom
light	light	light	
light	dark footsteps	blessing	
freedom	common heritage	all law	
purposes	love	territorially	
green green	love	exceeds	
white exploitation	technology	shrinks	
abundant	lapis lazuli	poor blue	
blue freedom of	copper	blue responsibility for	
cobalt trade	nickel zones	sovereign	
temptation	Anthropocene	exclusive white white	
white	provision	white white	
high-seas	dark geology	dark resources	
green	walking	black	
indigo	walking	black	
lapis lazuli	natural		

p   r   o   l   o   n   g   a   t   i   o   n

indigo blue b   a   s   e   l   i   n   e

Acknowledgements

'beginnings of bluegreen' was made possible by the performances and recordings of Tom Docherty, Hope Doherty, Jeremy Hardingham, Olivia Scott-Berry, Paige Smeaton, and Molly Vogel, and the support of the Judith E. Wilson Fellowship, Faculty of English, University of Cambridge.

'Azure Noise and Kinetic Syntax' was originally commissioned by the National Centre for Writing and British Council for the International Literature Showcase with the support of Arts Council England.

Sources for 'Spindrift Silences': Ursula Le Guin, *The Left Hand of Darkness* (London: Macdonald Science Fiction, 1969). Diego Marani, *New Finnish Grammar*. Translated by Judith Landry (Cambridge: Dedalus, 2011). Dylan Thomas, *Under Milk Wood* (London: J.M. Dent & Sons Ltd., 1962).

'Odyssey Response' was written in response to a commission from the actor Christopher Kent and pianist Gamal Khamis for their narrative recital *Odyssey – words and music of finding home*, premiered in November 2019.

'Windrush Reflections' was commissioned by Poet in the City and the British Library for Collections in Verse. A response to *Windrush: Songs in a Strange Land* and the communities of South Leeds. Inspiration for 'Windrush Lineage': Mahadai Das, *A Leaf in His Ear: Selected Poems* (Leeds: Peepal Tree Press, 2010). Sources for 'Caribbean Cento': collage of Lord Kitchener; Lord Beginner;

British Nationality Act 1948; Andrew Marr and Theresa May, 30/09/2018 interview, BBC transcript; Wilson Harris; Una Marson; V.S. Naipaul; Samuel Selvon; Michael Smith. Sources for 'Windrush Leeds Cento': collage of original material by participants in events in Leeds.

'A Short Prayer to Coffee' was written for performance at the launch of Helen Mort and Aaron Meskin, *Opposite: Poems, Philosophy and Coffee* (Scarborough: Valley Press, 2019), at the Hyde Park Book Club in Leeds.

'Landfall' mentions Reginald Bell's stained glass windows (1936), created and installed in memory of Margaret Gordon Harker in Blofield Church, Norfolk.

'In Praise of Birds' is a response to the memory of participating via improvisation in Caroline Bergvall's 'Conference (After Sweeney)' at the International Literary Festival in Dublin (May 2019).

'Odyssey Response' and 'In Praise of Birds' have been published in *PN Review*.

Sources for 'A Short Prayer to Oceans, by Erasures': Kamau Brathwaite, 'Bermudas', in *Born to Slow Horses* (Connecticut: Wesleyan University Press, 2005). Davor Vidas (2018). 'The Law of the Sea for a New Epoch?', in Stefanie Hessler (ed.) *Tidalectics: Imagining an oceanic worldview through art and science* (London and Massachussetts: MIT Press).

Reading, listening, and thanks: Leila Capildeo; Douglas Caster and the University of Leeds, for the Douglas Caster Cultural

Fellowship in Poetry (2017-19); Leeds Central Library; Dewsbury Road Library, Leeds; Ann Wilson and the SLATE Charity Group, Leeds; Becky Cherriman and Artlink West Yorkshire; Thahmina Begum and Health for All women's group, Leeds; the islanders on Lindisfarne; fellow sea swimmers in Dún Laoghaire, Inishbofin, St Andrews, and Tobago; Belmont Exotic Stylish Sailors; Jack Belloli; Tessa Berring; Mary Anne Clark and Dominic Leonard; Martin Colthorpe; Ian Duhig; Barbara Graziosi and Johannes Hauptbold; Chris Gribble; Selina Guinness and Colin Graham; Maggie Harris; Idara Hippolyte; Sharon Millar; Ghazal Mosadeq; Vivek Narayanan; Nat Raha; Judy Raymond; Gemma Robinson; The Mighty Shadow; Claire Stone; Jeremy Noel-Tod; Hanna Tuulikki; John Whale; Emily Wilson.

www.ingramcontent.com/pod-product-compliance
Lightning Source LLC
Chambersburg PA
CBHW021134080526
44587CB00012B/1285